ZADAR

FOR PAT

ZADAR

ALEXANDER TAYLOR

Ziesing Brothers Publishing
768 MAIN ST.
WILLIMANTIC, CONN.
06226

ACKNOWLEDGEMENT is gratefully made to the following magazines in which some of these poems first appeared: BOTTEGHE OSCURA, CONNECTICUT FIRESIDE, THE FAR POINT, FIDDLEHEAD, THE FINE ARTS MAGAZINE, FLOATING OPERA, KAYAK, MAINE EDITION, THE MALAHAT REVIEW, THE MASSACHUSETTS REVIEW, THE MEDITERRANEAN REVIEW, THE NEW YORK TIMES, THE OCCUM RIDGE REVIEW, THE PENNY PAPER, POETRY NOW, POETRY PILOT, 13 TEMPLE, THE WEST COAST REVIEW, and THE WORMWOOD REVIEW.

FRONTISPIECE by RICHARD WOLF

This book was brought to completion with the support of the Connecticut Commission on the Arts through the Connecticut Foundation for the Arts. I am grateful for their help.

My special thanks to James Scully, without whose encouragement this book would probably not have been finished. I also owe him a deep debt of gratitude for numerous helpful critical comments over the past ten years.

But most of all: This Book Is For Pat.

FIRST EDITION

ISBN: 0-917488-00-8

CONTENTS

BLACK STONE UPON A BLACK STONE

(With apologies to Cesar Vallejo)

I will die in Willimantic
between an ash can and a broken bottle,
waiting for dawn,
dreaming of foreheads and cards,
of ice cream and whiskey.

I will think of beautiful words to say
as I'm going
but no one will listen
because the game will still be playing
because the music won't have stopped.

I will die in Willimantic
as the pigeons are starting to flutter,
edging and rustling toward morning.
I will die on a Thursday,
my pockets turned inside out,
shouting:
    God! You made me miss the whole weekend!

SAYING GOODBYE

(For Mel and Beverly)

We were always saying goodbye.
Our departures band-aids ripped from flesh,
the tearing of hangnails.

We were always saying
"Let's be rational!"
"Let's think this thing through!"
as though love were algebra.

We were always saying goodbye
then rushing back to each other,
hysterically making love till morning,
tumbling back into ourselves,
asleep under the climbing sun.

I'll never understand:
we were always saying goodbye.
And now we've said it for good
I miss you and I'm glad you've gone
out of my love forever,
crocodile love,
hangnail,
betrayers and lovers.

SHEILA

Sweet nymph
rolling on the floor
biting his belly.
Even here, among the drunks,
in the dregs of the evening
you make a spectacle of yourself.

MONOLOGUE BY THE WINDOW

Your card came, a pinched bruise: "Please mail my coat.
I'm fine." Unsigned. Just the figure of a boat
sketched in beneath to recall those days
we sailed the Catspaw up and down the bays
of Connecticut, or drifted by the shore
in a dinghy, spent lovers on the floor.
The sun smoulders on the sandalwood.
Dust clouds the air; the smell of stale food
lingers in the kitchen. I glance through
a pile of mail, thankful for things to do,
brush a cobweb from bronze Venus who stares
tragically, giving herself airs.

Down by the brook, black branches cast their leaves
into the water, neither bread nor pennies;
this fall will not be proverbial.
For the first time I see the hawk-topped hill
shorn of its dressing, hugely naked,
and note the hedgehog's burrow. I never did
follow the simplest lines of self-protection.
So trees fall, lichen grows, punks sprout infection
and the pied genius of decay hangs upon
grizzly ribs. Things to do, or yet to come
buzz like dying flies within my head;
dusting, dishes, your coat, my narrow bed.

STRANGE ISLANDS

Why is it always at the hour of dusk
I see your pale face above the prow
of my small boat, whose task
is enormous, rowing toward those few
Strange Islands that recede before us?

It creaks and shudders on the choppy waters.
Framed in your jet hair--a perfect darkness--
is what these eyes strain to see, features
of a loved one, weary hearted,
gathered in a dream of yours.

Lucky the water, upon whose mirror
the boat glides and is cleanly forgotten.
There perfect stillness gathers, not fears
rising in stormy dreams to threaten
your image, drifting further than any island.

WHAT WAS REAL

What was real was not the midnightfarm
with blue flames eating up the fireplace
nor the fear driving our two lusts together,
the crash of flint and steel to coax a spark,
but the terrible outward drifting,
the mind flying further and further the body
and the knowledge that our thoughts will reinstall
this mythical farm, years later, like an old movie.

THE BROKEN WINDOW

In the quiet hours before dawn
you click up the sidewalk
like a clock.
I'm up here--a rusty anchor.
My tongue swells;
beads of sweat
cling like glycerine.

Unable to answer,
knowing for sure
you'll find the broken window,
I watch the blood ooze
from the hand
that opened the door
we'd both agreed
should be forbidden me.

How long since I last saw you?
How long since I came here
to find you gone,
and in a rage
crashed into this cell,
this silence,
to sit bemused
on your run-down sofa?
You cry up the stair:
Who's there? Who's up there?
Ah my chickadee,
my flaming darling,
I wish I knew.

MUMS

Outside the window the hardy mums sway in the chill wind,
        the raw November gusts.
Like us these few outlast the long intemperate summer.
        They hold their white heads up
as if they too had memories, as if they too had loved
        and watched the season end.
O lover and friend, so many things tug us apart.

The waters of different oceans soothe us now. Still I see
        white mums in the morning
nodding their heads in unison along the old stone wall--
        and then I like to think
if I outlive my time, fumbling like the old, senile
        and precious grandmothers,
I'd climb into the attic and end it with a shot--
        the same for love's end, but
chances are we'll cling to the wind, as these do now.

MARCH WALK

Walking across the campus
I saw them, like the long tail of a kite,
curving above the buildings, the birds,
a thick brushstroke quivering in the blue.

Twilight at the end of March, and cold.
And then they came sweeping in again, circling,
or else it was another flock, their twitterings
rising and falling, their wings madly flailing the air.

At Mirror Lake I saw where they were heading,
wheeling and turning above the tips of the evergreens
on the little island; hesitating, falling like grain
into the branches. Nearer, I heard the gargantuan
                              heartbeat.

CHEE, chee, chee, CHEE. Louder than a trillion
                              crickets,
and still circling in, thousands of them
and I thought of you, our vivid flock of days,
our staggering vibrant music, there in the cold twilight.

AFTER CHAGALL

I feel my love floating
above my head,
she bends her long neck down,
she kisses my lips,
arched as she is
over the living room,
holding a handful of flowers--
the whirling worlds of color
                climb, combine
with touch taste sound--
this body of love,
this living expectancy.

IN THE KITCHEN

Tracking you down in the kitchen
I catapult you off your feet
and simultaneously you leap into the air
and wrap your legs around my hips
gaze down on me
(those blue-green eyes with flecks of gold!)
as though I were your swing,
your trapeze,
your jaunty tightwire
taut with excitement,
and your warmth
commands my acrobatic heart
to keep on tumbling for you.
Whirling you around
I see your lips descend
to catch my lips
and feel your flying hair
electrify my neck, my face.
Gladdened, exhilarated, I
keep whirling and whirling
listening to the blood's applause.

SUSAN: LEARNING TO RIDE HER TWO WHEELER

Cautious as a cat
that's used eight careless lives
she gingerly wobbles
a few feet and stops.

I tell her
she must go fast
to keep her balance,
that the slower she goes
the more dangerous.
But she is having
none of this.

Ah but the day comes
when she'll spin the world
beneath those glinting wheels
and break the balance
of my heart.

A TALE FOR CHIDIOCK

We look to the hills,
planning conquests
in the tall pines,
the ore-laden mountains,
forseeing schemes
for the hearth centered house,
the well-governed city;
we stare over the gathering heads,
over the spikes of the gate
and spin such threads
as Ariadne gave to Theseus--
thus we cannot hear
the click and plummet
of the guillotine.

PORTRAIT

No angel called,
only certain nights
when dawn came on
gently effacing the stars
& I was breathing
the pure Connecticut air
alone on the back steps
shaking off the alcohol
standing by the lilacs
watching in fascination
black branches on the apple tree
turn pink & then softly
the first birds begin to twitter.

SHEILA DRIFTING

One shadow moving on the bedroom wall,
one thick candle on the bedside table,
its flickering tongue of light bends and leaps,
but cannot fill the room, though far down
the valley an owl shifts, narrows its lids,
fixing on the speck of yellow.
She lets her mind drift upon her distances,
sees the cross-timbered cottage in Holland,
touches his face there in the dark, and feels
a tongue that didn't speak but darted across
the roof of her mouth; then, then there was room
enough for the heady play of their lives,
she could hear the hum of the beehive near
their low voices murmuring as they faced
on the pillow, and filled and touched
and moved again.
           Dark, dark the forest of her hair,
the red tongue of flame roaring in her ear
in a time below sea-level when she rocked the bed.

SHEILA'S MORNING AFTER

She stands before the mirror
brushing her teeth, vigorously,
thinking: Last night he was
a mad airplane diving upon
my breasts, whirling through
the tangled clouds of my hair.
Brushing her hair, she thinks:
O yes, and last night he was
a deepdiving submarine
plumbing my depths, churning
and driving me until I was all
foam, till I was Venus new-born
swirling in a whirlpool, singing
the songs of the whales, the dolphins'
cry as I wrapped him in my mist
of love, kissed his electricity away.

She stands before the mirror
in which the bedroom behind her
shimmers in the twilight of dawn,
a backwards world; behind her
the passion the flight of angels.
It is as though a sleek jet
has made a bumpy landing,
blowing two tires. On the pillow
his unshaven face, smug, smiling
in sleep. He has returned to his own
center, circles under his eyes.

In the mirror she sees him
twisted, a wrecked car, his arm
over the edge, his mouth open, his

tousled hair against the creased and
rumpled pillow. She thinks: I
wrapped him in my octopus love,
I whispered my heart in his ear.
There was the thrill of flesh and pistons,
the fierce apocalypse annihilating
all. And now pausing before the mirror
she remembers his dictaphone
voice, and she watches him, sprawled
among the tangled blankets and sheets
who soon must rise and leave, and come
back, sometime, only he knows when.

LATE EVENING CONVERSATION

I love my husband, she says,
it's just that we think
so differently, we're separated
but we still see each other,
and we're really in love but
just can't live together any more.
Do you understand?   O lady I do,
it seems quite simple to me
who am in love with two women
and finding myself in you.

THE SEVERED HEAD

Professor Guillotine was wrong.
This agony is hardly just a cold sensation.
And I can hear!
I can hear the gurgling sound of my attorney.
He too got more than he expected.

But not even to feel the quivering of my body!
Or watch the flow of blackening blood,
or floating, sing my own elegy.

Someone hold up my head. I want to see!

Whose fingers in my hair? There now I'm rising.
The priest's red face! His stubby fingers
Make the sign. I swing outward
And back to my body again.

Then they close the basket.

Darkness, and the veins hammering.
Darkness, and the running blood.
Darkness, and the jolting of the cart.
Darkness, and the film of my eyes thickening
As this improbable journey begins.

LETTER

Dear Jim,
another off and on again day,
a bit of sun, a bit of rain,
no wonder Hamlet had his problems.
We are also having
our ups and downs.
Sometimes the circus men
selling tickets to the roller coaster
have strange smiles.
The owner sits in the back room
counting his money;
the performers are underpaid,
but still go on.
It is only then they can forget
the whole show isn't worth it.
Still, there are always those rare moments
of incomparable gesture.
To the strains of piano and strings
the lady with the umbrella
sashays along the taut wire.
Later she is sad.
We are all sad.
As you once said
it may be man is incapable
of being happy--
except in flashes, I would add.
When the strings of bright lights
blink out
and the walks and lawns are deserted
and an awful stillness
presses down
until we feel flattened like butterflies,

we lie there trying to figure it out.
Or a way out.
At that moment
there is nothing we can do
to help each other--
except just be there,
if we're wanted.

THREE O'CLOCK

It moves gently
like March fog
obscuring the trees
and making the highways dangerous

as though someone travelling very fast
suddenly desires to relinquish the wheel
and lie down among the dark stones forever.

MAD CHATTER

You were a strange bird--
each time someone got out
you said, "Don't worry,
you'll be back.
They always come back."
We laughed. It was all part
of the mad chatter.
When you left
you took my dollar--
I never did see the wine
you swore you'd smuggle past the nurse.
It doesn't matter.
I suppose you found a strike
or someone took it off you playing cards.

I recall our compulsive talk
as we looked across Hartford
through the mesh
of the hospital windows.
I roared over the thin red head
you continued against all odds
trying to make--each week
holding hands, kissing, and then
they shot her head so full of electrons
she couldn't even remember your face,
and you were back to scratch,
cursing Thales, Gilbert, Galvani, and Franklin.

You'd had yourself circumcised
to get your dope,
a comic ploy, we thought,
as you kept saying, "Agh, come on

Doc, the pain, the pain," and practiced
walking wide-legged down the narrow hall.
In the end they threw you out.
You were certain
that there was only one cure
for your disease--
even the Lexington, Kentucky headshrinkers
couldn't get you off the hook
(and they were hooked themselves).
Your cure was my fear.
What was I doing there?
Here in grey Danish weather
I stare across the frozen strait,
hardly knowing where the ice ends
and the water starts. Near shore
its stippled surface changes
in the morning light. Soon the whole strait
may be slush
if the lumbering ships keep on crushing ice.
Sitting in an old chair, wheezing,
trying not to smoke,
I wonder what's become of you
these five years.
Did you die on schedule
or are you in some damp
gas station rest room,
cold and sweaty, followed by cops,
unfixing with trembling hands
the rusty mystical needle
you'd taped last week
under the grimy wash basin?

WAITING FOR SLEEP TO HAPPEN

Even at Canaveral they make mistakes--
my switched lines keep the buzzers going,
small sounds magnify the dark.
This strangeness of mine, this body I keep around
for its occasional convenience, loves the night.
This owl-like contraption
won't obey the simplest laws of nature
or respond to pills or beer.
Never mind, I love you anyway,
my grotesque imperfect bumbler.
You're like the worn-out sweaters
I refuse to throw away.

PLAYING GIN RUMMY WITH SHEILA

Shuffling the cards
like a sharpie,
creating a red waterfall
that never spills its boundaries,
nevertheless you still wear
the madonna's secret placidness
and
    turn up a smile.
But those tight bandages
braceleting your wrists!

VAN GOGH'S EAR

The sun bursts through the clouds
on the cry of a rooster,
coppers the green leaves of the hedge--
a fresh wind up from the sea--
straw roofs shine in morning light,
red poppies wave in the barley--
weeds
that spatter the field with blood.
High up in the air
riding in the wind
a lark goes crazy
singing and singing.
The bees buzz like flies.
Madness is always near,
the witch lady
married to joy.
Vincent, I think of you,
I think of your ear,
I go forth to meet my frenzy.

MINNIE

You said
"Don't worry,
the flies will all be dead
by morning." That was after
you'd thrown Harry's pants
and two tile ashtrays
into the washing machine--together.
The pants looked like
they'd been used for shotgun practice.
"O.K., Minnie," Sam said, knowing
your compulsion for hoarding,
your knack for kleptomania,
"I'm missing a book."
"Well write it all down on a paper,
I'm busy now. I've got too much
wet shoes, and I have to walk
the water out of them."
We never could come out on top.
Once Lois yelled, "Hey Minnie, you're
wearing your sweater inside out!"
"I know I am, stupid,
that's so the lint
won't get on the right side."
Later Willie tried his flip lip
& winked & bowed at us & said
"Hey Minnie, you look like my
grandmother." "If you feed them,"
you shot back, "they live longer.
You've been all around the world
and that's as far as you'll get.
I'd keep right on going."

Still you grabbed your chance
when it came time to leave
the hilarious house of the mad.
You allowed you had to get home
when we said we couldn't afford to let you go.
"I've got a dog who misses me.
When I wash him he changes colors
every time he moves."

KAFKA'S APPLE

> "A sad tale's best for winter; I have
> one of sprites and goblins."

Kafka's apple haunts me now,
the hard fruit bedded in flesh
deep and gangrenous. We crawl
around in winter's fulness,
the world transfroms us at its wish.
Ah, a dog, Sir, a dog can snarl,
but we have chewed our fangs to stubs.

High notes from bow and string,
a deep rush of imagining,
yet you are sad
that winter comes. It drives me mad,
black seeds rattling in an apple core.
Who knows the song?
Over hump-backed bridges footsteps clang.

Yet sometimes there was music in your eyes:
I saw there distant villages, the bourne
below the walls of the towering city,
there, where the water's green
embraces the green of the tree.

THE FOUR DAYS' DIET

One more to go.
My stomach's a peach pit
and here I am reading to Future Hope
nervous that I might suddenly pass out
fall down on the rug
or break a chair.

It's your fault van der Velde,
sticking me with a daily eight ounces of meat
and water (all I can drink--with ice cubes for dessert),
but nothing else, no coffee, beer, whiskey,
vegetables, soda, cake, sundaes, bread, shrimp,
milk, wine, or cookies, no not even toothpaste
                              or a toothpick.

Your test's
for my own good no doubt,
but I'm finding it hard
to go in for delayed gratification
when I'd much rather go in for a meal.

Ak, ya, you injected your cliche:
"It's impossible to enjoy the good things
without ever having been without them"
(as you discovered in Holland during the war).
I wanted to pick up your stehoscope
and blow "Shrimp Boat's Are A'coming" in your ear.

Driving here tonight the hills looked like
Big Rock Candy Mountain, the streams were

the color of wine, and when I saw
a well-endowed blonde swinging across the street
I didn't think of brick outbuildings,
I kept thinking about milk.

Bless you, Dr. van der Velde, you are right,
but I'm just not used to it,
never having lived under war conditions
although always during a war.

Though my mind's been screwed up
frequently, my stomach's always been full,
and even if Friday's traditionally fast day,
after you needle the blood out of my arm
I'm going to stuff my stomach so deliciously
                          so slowly full
it will make the most splendiferous Roman banquet
seem like a Bangladesh hors d'oeuvre.

LIKE IT WAS

Whistling up the path
past the forsythia
eager for the day,
up into the meadows
for a crack at ploughing
or for a few hours
roughing your fingers on stone
as the wall took shape,
before the ships set sail
from the harbor,
before the town was sacked
and you came home in garlands,
before the terror and the myth,
before the terror of the myth,
after which you seemed always smaller,
confronted by the quizzical glance,
caught by the questions of the young
or the inquiring look of the elders.
You will have to die
to benefit the legend.

APOLOGIA

> "All I can say to those I meet:
> 'Try and make it to Cold Mountain.'"
>
> Gary Snyder
>
> "To reduce material desires does not
> always bring peace of mind. In order
> to live in peace, spiritual desires
> must also be reduced."
>
> KAPPA, Akutagawa

Good poet, I was making it
toward Cold Mountain.
The vistas were thrilling my heart
but I was treading the way,
driven by a primal urge.
The white peaks glittered.
I lifted my face to the cold, pure wind.

I met her by the fountain
in the upper provinces.
Her yes collected forests
and harmless birds. I forgot Cold Mountain.
In that clearing I built our house
and entered my children's
green childhood.
Often making love we saw the moon
shine over us
and sometimes drifting down to sleep
I dreamed its shadowed face
riding over the cold peaks. Soon

they were grown, those children,
but the children of the town
had entered my schoolroom.
Cold Mountain, always you shone
in the distance.

Then domestic war:
children from dark streets,
from old buildings where rats
scurried, came here
and sat in a circle, reciting poems.
Their quick thoughts
entered my flesh,
their sparrow joys--
and Cold Mountain glittered.

Gradually
a war in Asia
based on a lie.
Then even exile would have been
a strange blessing,
but no, I lay abed
dreaming of you, writing letters
and lectures, and half-made poems.

Cold Mountain, often I think of going,
but always a jewelled toad squats at my ear:
"This one or that one needs your blood."

LETTER TO AN EXILE

Remember the quiet ponds
in yesterday's mountains?

(Those moments that glide
like fish into the shadows!)

Today rain swept the dust
from the tiles of our roof.

The air plunges into my lungs.
I have polished the silver

and straightened your study.
Everything is ready

for the sound of your steps.

THE RETURN

          will be certain.
I, your hopeless boomerang,
curving back to you
& with a quick confident gesture
you reach out to me:
it is as though a bird
has lightly settled
on your hand.

ELEGY IN APRIL

My brother, our death,
      both cold and warm winds blow
through town this average April--
five months since you lost your breath
      in one wild plunge.
Well, yours was the choice to make.

Those fears that shamed me
      are gone now, and I awake
some mornings not having had
one dream of you. You tamed me
      by tumbling down:
Your death was my looking glass.

Winds spin, and I breathe
      deeply. Darknesses pass.
I watch your children, your flesh,
race through grass where locusts seethe,
      not falling down
but running out where they can breathe.

A FEW WORDS IN THE LATE AFTERNOON

You remembered me as the young man who burned
                                    his poems.
I remembered you a bony bewitching beauty
in a black lace swimsuit by her greenwater pool.
friends of friends--nothing more.

I remember how your clear blue eyes would shine
as you spoke your poems, leaning and swaying,
(poetry that was a fire in your throat)
how you reined and channelled the terror
and tore free from the arms of darkness,
from the obscure angular figure
who broke into your dreams with phosphorescent eyes,
and all about were vampires, ghouls...

Jealous of Sylvia's suicide, shocked, hurt,
and sorry--like a scar under your eyelid--
you went on, tried to outwit
your private furies.

So you made it at last, Anne,
curled up in your quick-idling car
comfy and warm,
a downy bear inside her winter tree.

AMERICAN GOTHIC

Madness with its
baroque candelabra
burning the cobwebs
in the tinder house
O lovely woman
lie by my side
your skin shining
with sweat, your knees
like apples, my woods
are burning and the castle
shakes in the thunderous
air--nowhere, nowhere
scream the jays, as
random violence
in the sleek guise
of Huck Finn and
Tom Sawyer hack
my son to pieces, my
daughter violate
and cast down
by the reeling shore
while the oiled machinery
whirs, whirs--
escalators and elevators
riding up the mad blue air.
O lovely woman
lie by my side
your tragic tongue
circles my globe, generations
hum in ecstacy
  intense angels expand
their flashing amours

we rise in flame
like the warehouse
burning our sorrows away
Come, dive like the kingfisher
upon me, moisten me
with your force, your
milk-breathing mouth
for Death is a pale woman
wearing a necklace of seaweed,
her sinuous thighs flash
like algae
in the cold currents of dawn
now I fall upon
the warm banks of your body
digging the miraculous grave
tomorrow I put on
the straitjacket that is my life.

ZADAR

Go from me!
Hurry!

Break from me.
Look how the swallows break
exploding over the hillside
like my scattered directions.

Go from me now.
All day a silence has been slowly building
where the worm sadness gnaws
at the fount of our joy,
where the sane agreement of our flesh
promises madness.

You seem sad, you said.
No, no, it's the heat,
I'm happy, I'm happy.

For three days the firm fit of our bodies,
our jointed talk,
brought us into the safe garden,
the secure citadel.
Just try not to think of the tumbling of the walls!
Jericho's in our blood and in our lives.

You said, Why are you so good to me?
It shook me like a fever
to see you turn on the balcony
and smile, thankful as a saint,
and I thought the thoughts
I had so feared from you.
I stood stunned because I stood
outside the windows of my reason
like a weary stranger.

We played with the honey of love,
the stinging bees of desire,
and now relief--a thankful sigh--
waits round the corner.
Why were you so good to me?

An anguish is stabbing my joy.
Go quickly!